The Amazing Christian Life

Ten Transforming Truths

Cynthia Kirchner

Lasting Legacy Books
Federal Way, WA

Cynthia Kirchner/Lasting Legacy Books
1911 SW Campus Dr. #684
Federal Way, WA 98023
www.lastinglegacybooks.com

Book Layout ©2015 BookDesignTemplates.com

Ordering Information:
Quantity sales. Special discounts are available on quantity purchases by corporations, associations, and others. For details, contact the "Special Sales Department" at the address above.

ISBN 978-1-946239-06-8

Dedicated to the ladies of Faith Baptist Church

I love you all!

Contents

Preface

To the reader

Welcome to *The Amazing Christian Life*. Before you begin, it is important that I share a few thoughts with you.

We live in a time when it seems almost everyone is a critic or a censor. My desire in writing this book is to share with you the positive side of the Christian experience. Honestly, I have never gotten over the joy and wonder of God's love and goodness. My life has been transformed. The changes didn't happen at all once; the whole thing has been a process. Every day of my life, I discover something new and wonderful that God has provided just for my benefit. My earnest desire is that others also enjoy this amazing Christian life.

Christ's followers are sometimes defined by what we are against. I believe that the things we are for are what should define the Christian life, as they are what define our God. Because God loves us, He hates the sin that harms us. Because God loves families, He hates immorality and adultery. Because God loves grace and truth, He hates corruption, lying and deception. We must never forget that God's love for His children is immense and likewise, His hatred for sinful behavior beckons an equal amount of disdain.

I have seen up close, the results of sin: the untimely death of loved ones gone too soon from alcoholism, drug abuse, divorce and abandonment. I have had lies and hatred directed towards me, just as they have probably been flung towards you. In view of God's abundant blessings, all of those things fade into obscurity. I see each day as an adventure that I can't wait to experience.

Satan's lie has always been that God is not good therefore, He withholds good things from us. Many people believe this today, as they mock the very truth that would rescue them from their own destruction. If in a small way, the light of truth and hope could shine through this little book to those who are disappointed and disillusioned, all of the tears and travail would be more than worthwhile.

Join me as we discover *The Amazing Christian Life*.

Cindy

Introduction

The Amazing Christian Life

When you hear the word amazing, what comes to mind? Is it just another overused word that no longer elicits a response, or does it spark emotion in you? What does amazing mean? It refers to those things above our level of ability, outside the realm of our possibilities, and that which exceeds all of our life experience. Amazing is those things beyond our comprehension. Paul describes it as, "exceeding abundantly above all that we ask or think, according to the power that worketh in us."[1] Let's consider describing our lives in Christ in this way along with well-deserved synonyms such as astonishing, astounding, remarkable, incredible, marvelous, and miraculous.

---

1   Ephesians 3:20

The length, breadth, and depth of Almighty God is incomprehensible; therefore, some people discount the reality of His existence. This line of thinking is counter intuitive to the very idea of God. If we could comprehend God, He would not be God. He would simply be a product of our own imaginations. God's wisdom and ways are unsearchable and beyond our understanding.[2]

Not only is God amazing in His person, His power, His plan, and His purpose, but God is also amazing in His personal communication with mankind. It is overwhelming to consider that the God of all creation would take an intimate and personal interest in you or me, one of billions of individuals. It is amazing that He, who created the immense universe, as well as the infinitesimal particles of the atom, counts the hairs on our heads as they turn gray and fall out. This connection, this relationship with the Divine, is the essence of the amazing Christian life.

This little book cannot begin to describe all of the riches available to us, but our hope is that it will cause us to be more aware of the miraculous gifts we have been given. Many, perhaps most of us live far below our God-given privileges. The Bible tells us of the incredible blessings God has for us, but we disregard them believing they are meant for others and not for us. We can find assurance that His promises apply to all of us, when we truly believe Paul's words in 1 Corinthians 2:9, *"But as it is written, Eye hath not seen, nor ear heard, neither have entered into the heart*

---

2   Romans 11:33

of man, the things which God hath prepared for them that love him."

Is your life thrilling? Are you filled with expectancy and excitement as you face each new day?

Is your communion with God sweet and uninterrupted? Join me as we discover anew our inheritance as God's dear children. Come, and let us claim our rightful position as joint heirs in Christ.[3]

On the following pages, we will explore ten amazing aspects of the life we have in Christ:

Amazing Salvation – God's Plan

Amazing Love – God's Acceptance

Amazing Grace - God's Riches

Amazing Answers – God's Response

Amazing Truth – God's Revelation

Amazing Calling – God's Anointing

Amazing Fruit – God's Abundance

Amazing Communion – God's Presence

Amazing Wisdom – God's Guidance

Amazing Worship – Our Response

---

3   Romans 8:17

The more we learn about Him, there is no question that to know God is to love Him.

CHAPTER ONE

Amazing Salvation

God's Plan

Think back with me to the day you accepted God's gift of eternal life. Do you remember where you were? Who was with you? What verses did you obey? What emotions did you feel? How much did you really know and understand at that moment? Have you ever taken the time to write out the story of your salvation? I encourage you to do so. Not only will you again rejoice in God's goodness to you personally, but you will also leave a testimony for the benefit of others.

A genuine conversion experience results in a transformed life; a life with the potential to impact hundreds, thousands, maybe millions of lives. Take Dwight L. Moody for example; it is estimated that Moody led over one million souls to a saving knowledge of Jesus Christ. Moody had resisted the Gospel for a period of time. One afternoon, his Sunday School teacher, Edward Kimble, determined to visit him where he worked as a shoe salesman. His testimony follows:

> Going over to Dwight in the back of the shoe store, "I placed my hand on his shoulder, leaned over, and placed my foot on a shoe box."

> Kimball looked into Dwight's eyes and "asked him to come to Christ, who loved him and who wanted his love and should have it."

> Dwight's struggle came to a head, and he surrendered his will to God's will and came to Christ through Kimball's invitation.

> "My plea was a very weak one," Kimball observed later, "but I was sincere." He also realized, "The young man was just ready for the light that broke upon him. For there, at once, in the back of that shoe store in Boston, Dwight gave himself and his life to Christ."

> The following morning as he left his room, Dwight's happiness and peace knew no bounds. The wide grin on his face and the fresh sparkle in his big brown eyes reflected his newfound joy. He sensed, "The old sun shone a good deal brighter

then it ever had before—I felt that it was just smiling upon me; and as I walked out upon Boston Common and heard the birds singing in the trees, I thought they were all singing a song to me."

As he marched along, it seemed all creation cheered him on his way, and he sensed that "I had not a bitter feeling against any man, and I was ready to take all men to heart." (Harvey, *Moody* 28-30)

John James Muir tells of the salvation experience of Charles Finney, a powerful revival preacher of the Second Great Awakening, in the book *President Finney of Oberlin, The Family Treasury*.

He came, however, to the conclusion that the Bible was the "Word of God." He was deeply moved. He must settle the question whether he would choose Christ or the world; he must settle it soon.

An inward voice seemed to ask him in his misery: "What are you waiting for? Did you not promise to give your heart to God? And what are you trying to do? Are you endeavouring to work out a righteousness of your own?"

Just at that point the reality and fulness of the atonement broke upon his mind. He saw that, instead of having to do anything himself, he had to submit himself to the righteousness of God in Christ. "Gospel salvation seemed to me to be an offer of something to be accepted, and that it was full and complete, and that all that was necessary on my part was to get my own consent to give up my sins and accept Christ."

He had stopped in the street during the time "this distinct revelation had stood before his mind." The question came to him: Would he accept this offer of salvation to-day? He replied: "Yes; I will accept it, or I will die in the attempt."

Personally, I was a child when I first heard and understood the Gospel. I did not struggle with believing as some adults struggle. I believed and I received. God makes salvation so simple, even a child can understand it. God calls and we answer. But salvation is also so infinite; none of us comprehends it fully.

First, we do not comprehend how corrupt and deformed mankind became when Adam and Eve disobeyed God. At our very core, we are desperately wicked. Jeremiah wrote, *"The heart is deceitful about all things, and desperately wicked: who can know it?"*[4] We, as humans, like to believe that we can be good in our own power. Some even believe that we are born good. Our parents always told us to be good, but specifically, what did they want us to do? I remember trying to attain that title. I tried to be nice to my sister. I tried not to argue when it was time to go to bed. I tried not to

---

4   Jeremiah 17:9

fight over the toys. But I always failed. Even as a child, I knew I was a sinner.

Paul said the same, only much more eloquently, when he expressed, *"For I know that in me (that is, in my flesh,) dwelleth no good thing: for to will is present with me; but how to perform that which is good I find not."*[5]

It is human nature to try to justify our misdeeds by saying, "This is just the way I am." Actually, that is a true statement, but it is hardly an acceptable excuse for our wicked thoughts and actions. David recognized the same thing, but he did not use it as justification. He was overwhelmed with his own sin when he said, *"Behold, I was shapen in iniquity; and in sin did my mother conceive me."*[6] We like to pretend that we would never do anything truly horrible, but when our emotions explode, and we are overcome with anger or hatred, we are stunned by our inherent evil capabilities. It is a tough reality to face and leaves us grappling with a sense of self-loathing and helplessness. This is the poison of sin that pollutes all of us.

Secondly, we cannot comprehend the utterly devastating consequences of our sin. We are finite. We cannot grasp eternity. We cannot imagine never-ending separation, suffering, the blackness of darkness for ever[7], or a place where *"the smoke of their torment that ascendeth up for ever and ever: where the wicked have no rest day nor night."*[8]

---

5   Romans 7:18
6   Psalm 51:5
7   Jude 13
8   Revelation 14:11

These are just two of the places in the Bible where eternity without God is described. In this life, we see glimpses of the darkest elements of the human soul, void of any knowledge of God. We are repulsed in horror at the images of the Nazi concentration camps. We are sickened by the beheading and abuses heaped on people by the terrorists of today. All of those atrocities are temporary. What unimaginable horrors can eternity hold for those who reject God and His Son? We cannot conceive of the wretchedness of a place where God is not.

Even at our most rebellious, we can feel God's presence and influence in this life. We know that *"He maketh his sun to rise on the evil and on the good, and sendeth rain on the just and on the unjust,"*[9] but, there is coming a day when this will no longer be the case. There is coming a time and a place of outer darkness, absent of His presence, where *"there shall be wailing and gnashing of teeth."*[10]

Thirdly, we cannot begin to comprehend the sacrifice the Lord Jesus Christ made for us, when He, *"...being in the form of God, thought it not robbery to be equal with God: But made himself of no reputation, and took upon him the form of a servant, and was made in the likeness of men: And being found in fashion as a man, he humbled himself, and became obedient unto death, even the death of the cross."*[11]

---

9   Matthew 5:45
10   Matthew 13:42
11   Philippians 2:6-8

Good-byes are hard on most people. None of us likes the thought of leaving. It is a great sacrifice when our soldiers leave home to go defend our freedom. It always brings tears to my eyes when

we see pictures of our troops, hugging their families as they return home. Separation is so painful. How much more did our Savior sacrifice leaving Heaven to suffer and die of us!

The Lord knew what awaited Him; while agonizing in the garden, He prayed, *"Father, if thou be willing, remove this cup from me: nevertheless not my will, but thine, be done. And there appeared an angel unto him from heaven, strengthening him. And being in an agony he prayed more earnestly: and his sweat was as it were great drops of blood falling down to the ground."[12]*

The greatest price our Savior paid was not separation from His glory in Heaven. His greatest agony was the moment of separation from His Father, when He became sin for us, and God the Father turned His face from God the Son.

"And about the ninth hour Jesus cried, with a loud voice, saying, Eli, Eli, lama sabachthani? that is to say, My God, my God, why hast thou forsaken me?"[13]

It is often said that salvation is free, but it is not free. It is offered to us at a great cost. Because He paid it all, we have nothing more to do except to receive it. We pay nothing, because He paid our debt in full.

---

12   Luke 21:41-44
13   Matthew 27:46

Let's not forget the absolute most amazing aspect of our Savior's sacrifice. He died for our sin, true, but according to Romans 14:9, *"For to this end Christ both died, and rose, and revived, that he might be Lord both of the dead and living."* Our Messiah defeated death and the grave, when He arose!

Jesus lived a sinless life. Because He was pure and perfect, He could be a sacrifice for our sin. He could pay the debt we owed, because He had no debt of His own. He also had to break the bonds of death. He had to demonstrate His power over death. We can confidently say, *"Because He lives, we shall also live!"* Paul writes about this mighty power in 1 Corinthians 15:54-44, when he declares, *"So when this corruptible shall have put on incorruption, and this mortal shall have put on immortality, then shall be brought to pass the saying that is written, Death is swallowed up in victory. O death, where is thy sting? O grave, where is thy victory?"*

Finally, we cannot begin to comprehend all the benefits we receive at the moment of salvation. Paul prayed for the Ephesians, that they might have some comprehension of the breadth and length and depth and height of what Christ has done for us. Ultimately, it is beyond our meager ability to comprehend it all, which is why Ephesians 3:17-19 states, *"That Christ may dwell in your hearts by faith; that ye, being rooted and grounded in love, May be able to comprehend with all saints what is the breadth, and length, and depth, and height; And to know the love of Christ, which passeth knowledge, that ye might be filled with all the fulness of God."*

We often use the example in Romans 6:23, *"For the wages of sin is death; but the gift of God is eternal life through Jesus Christ our Lord,"* to describe salvation as a gift. This simple illustration reveals a much deeper truth. Wages are something we earn, and death is what we earn for our sinfulness. Of course, we understand death as an end, a separation from life and hope and the presence of God. Salvation, on the other hand, is a gift. It is not something we earn. It is something we receive.

Imagine yourself walking on a deserted street, in the heat of the day, in mid-August. You have walked for miles searching for a gas station, since your car has stalled on the side of the rural road. You haven't eaten in hours and your last drink of anything was your morning coffee. Suddenly, a stranger appears, slows down their air-conditioned car, and pulls over beside you. Seeing your frustration and discomfort, they reach into the backseat and greet you with a tall bottle of water, dripping with cold condensation. The satisfaction of that first gulp? Unmatched.

Water is so easy to come by in our culture that we can't really fathom any extended period of time without it. As with most things in life, we usually don't appreciate what we have until we have gone without it. This is salvation. We do not realize the amazing value of the gift God has given to us until we consider what the hardships and victories of life would be like without it.

God gave Himself to us. He restored our relationship with Him. Salvation means that not only do we get to know Who He is, but we abide in Him! We start out separated from God because of our filthiness, and we end up enveloped in the vastness of His everlasting love.

Salvation is a gift we unwrap in layers, day by day. Imagine opening God's gift, taking it in your hands and turning it over, repeatedly. As you examine it from every angle, you find something new and different at each turn, amazed at its unlimited wonder. Jesus described it as being born again.[14] We are made new. Our old life passes away, and God gives us a new life to experience, in Christ.[15]

Reflections:

If you have never truly accepted Jesus Christ as your Savior and been forgiven of your sin, this is the first step on an amazing life journey. Jesus said, *"Behold, I stand at the door, and knock: if any man hear my voice, and open the door, I will come in to him, and will sup with him, and he with me."*[16] Why not invite Him to come in today, forgive your sin and give you eternal life in Him? Here is a sample prayer to help you begin.

"Dear Lord Jesus, I know I am a sinner. I believe you died for me. I invite you to come into my heart and life, and take away my sin. I trust you to lead me and guide me through this life and to take me to Heaven, to spend eternity with you, when I die. Amen."

If you prayed this prayer and would like more information on living a Christian life, please contact me at:

---

14   John 3:3-8
15   2 Corinthians 5:17
16   Revelation 3:20

cynthia@lastinglegacybooks.com. I would be so happy to hear from you and to send you a free New Testament and Bible Study Lessons. In the meantime, keep reading!

Throughout this book, we are going to unwrap more of the gems that fill our amazing Christian life. We could never exhaust the subject, but we will certainly enjoy the wonder of it as we journey together.

"For God so loved the world, that he gave his only begotten Son,

that whosoever believeth in him should not perish,

but have everlasting life."

John 3:16

CHAPTER TWO

Amazing Love

God's Acceptance

They say love makes the world go round. But, more accurately love made the world because, *"God is love; and he that dwelleth in love dwelleth in God, and God in him."*[17]

The word *love,* in the English language, is frequently used interchangeably with the word *like*. I love chocolate. I like peas. I love my home. I like my car. There are some languages that do not have a word for like; their word for love is the same as their word for like. To like something or to love someone is a matter of degrees. Many a poet, songwriter and romance novelist have attempted to describe love in varying degrees. Love is an

---

17   1 John 4:16

intangible; we all know how it feels and what it does to us, but words can never adequately describe it.

C.S. Lewis in his book, *The Four Loves*, notes that four different Greek words are translated love. Two of them are used explicitly, and the other two are alluded to, but never used, in the New Testament.

Storge is empathy, or family love. This word is not found in our Bible, but we find its essence throughout God's Word. It is the natural affection that a parent has for a child.

Jesus said, *"If a son shall ask bread of any of you that is a father, will he give him a stone? Or if he ask a fish, will he for a fish give him a serpent?"*[18] Parents love and care for their children. God's love is often compared to the love of a parent for a child, but it goes so much deeper than this.

Eros is romantic love. It is also not found in our Bible, but it is wonderfully described in the Song of Solomon. Here, a bride and a bridegroom describe their love for one another, voicing desires like, *"Let him kiss me with the kisses of his mouth: for thy love is better than wine."*[19]

God calls us His beloved, and He compares His love for us to that of a bridegroom coming to take his bride away. *"Behold, thou art fair, my beloved, yea, pleasant: also our bed is green,"*[20] As wonderful and enthralling as we know romantic love to be, God's

---

18   Luke 11:11
19   Song of Solomon 1:2
20   Song of Solomon 1:16

love for us runs deeper. Still, romantic love can wear away. God's love never can.

Phileo is brotherly love, or friendship. A Biblical example of this love is Jesus' friendship with Mary, Martha and their brother, Lazarus. In this passage, Mary and Martha send word to Jesus that Lazarus, whom He loved as a brother and a friend, is sick.[21] In another instance, Jesus refers to the disciples as His friends, telling them, *"Greater love hath no man than this, that a man lay down his life for his friends. Ye are my friends, if ye do whatsoever I command you."*[22]

As God's friends, we have a personal, loving relationship with Him, but God's love for us is even more profound than the love of an earthly friend. There is no greater love than the love God has for us! This brings us to the fourth love described in the Bible.

Agape is unconditional, sacrificial love. There is nothing you can do to make God love you any more; likewise, there is nothing you can do to make God love you any less. We did not earn God's love. God loves us because of Who He is, not because of who we are. His love is pursuant, *"We love him, because he first loved us,"*[23] He shows us His unconditional love in that, *"while we were yet sinners, Christ died for us."*[24]

Charles Wesley called this an amazing love in his hymn, "And Can It Be."

---

21   John 11:3
22   John 15:13-14
23   1 John 4:19
24   Romans 5:8

"And Can It Be"

Charles Wesley 1738

And can it be that I should gain

An interest in the Savior's blood?

Died He for me, who caused His pain—

For me, who Him to death pursued?

Amazing love! How can it be,

That Thou, my God, shouldst die for me?

God's amazing love never fails.

A well-read and highly educated theologian was asked, "What is the greatest Bible truth you have ever studied?" He replied, "Jesus loves me, this I know, for the Bible tells me so." Nothing transforms a life like the realization of God's undying love, and not only to His children as a part of the whole, but also uniquely as individuals. Even humanists recognize man's innate need to be loved. We were created in God's image, and God is love; therefore, *"Whoever does not know God does not know love, because God is love."*[25] We were created to love and to be loved.

Every loving human relationship is a reflection of God's love in our lives. When we are truly loved by another, we are accepted. Our faults, our foibles, our imperfections, our weaknesses and our foolish acts are overlooked and forgiven. All human love has its

---

25   1 John 4:8

limitations, but God's love is infinite. As we read in 1 Corinthians 13:13, *"And now abideth faith, hope, charity, these three; but the greatest of these is charity."* Love never fails. Is there anything more devastating than rejection, especially the rejection of one we've loved and whom we believed loved us? What makes Hell so horrendous is not merely the torment and suffering, but the eternal separation from God, from the source of all hope and all love.

This amazing love is the basis of God's acceptance. As children of God, we never have to be separated from God. He never rejects us and He doesn't merely tolerate us. He loves us so much that He guarantees we never have to worry about His love faltering, *"For I am persuaded, that neither death, nor life, nor angels, nor principalities, nor powers, nor things present, nor things to come, Nor height, nor depth, nor any other creature, shall be able to separate us from the love of God, which is in Christ Jesus our Lord."*[26]

What, then, should be our response to God's love? Because we truly understand love's depth and power, *"we ought also to love one another."*[27]

We should never forget that God sent His Son because He loves us. We, in turn, are meant to love others with the same love. God listens to our prayers and answers us. God understands us. God is always with us. God shares our sorrows and our joys. God speaks to us when we listen. The more conscious we are of God's love

---

26   Romans 8:28-29
27   1 John 4:11

for us, the more love we have to share with others. We prove that love by listening to others, trying to understand them, being present when they need us, mourning when they mourn, and celebrating when they celebrate. Max Lucado hit the nail on the head when he said, "The secret to loving is living loved."

The Lord commands us to love one another, to be kind, to forgive and to be tender hearted. We fulfill all of these things when we respond to the love God shows to us. If we are ever unsure of our duty as Christ's followers, we only need to remember John 13:34, *"A new commandment I give unto you, That ye love one another; as I have loved you, that ye also love one another."*

Fredrick Lehman found a verse scribbled on the wall of a patient's room in an asylum after the man was carried to his grave. The words are a translation of an Aramaic poem, "Haddamut", written ca. 1050 by Rabbi Meir of Worms, Germany. From the verse he wrote the following song.

"The Love of God"

Fredrick Lehman 1917

Could we with ink the ocean fill,

And were the skies of parchment made,

Were every stalk on earth a quill,

And every man a scribe by trade;

To write the love of God above

Would drain the ocean dry;

Nor could the scroll contain the whole,

Though stretched from sky to sky.

Oh, love of God, how rich and pure!

How measureless and strong!

It shall forevermore endure—

The saints' and angels' song.

In our darkest moments, the love of God shines the brightest. Some of the sweetest testimonies come from those facing the most difficult of trials. The realization that God loves me, "a sinner condemned unclean," gives us strength and hope that nothing else ever can.

One of the most joyful Christians I have ever known was my mother-in-law. Her smile was infectious. Looking at her and listening to her, one would never have guessed the abuse and suffering she had endured in life. As a child, her parents were involved in a satanic cult. Late at night when they met, she was often dragged from her bed and beaten by the participants. As a young woman, she left to marry a cruel and abusive husband, who later left her for another woman. Her marriage to my husband's father was a happy one, but she was then stricken with a paralyzing disease. Only a few years later, her husband died, leaving her a disabled widow.

When we visited her, not once did we find her missing an opportunity to sing praises to God. Everyone in her apartment complex knew her smile and song. On many occasions, she told me of the day God's love for her became personal. She'd always believed she deserved the abuse she had suffered. She saw herself as unloved and unlovely, until the realization of God's unconditional love flooded her heart and mind. It transformed her life. She got great joy from telling others, "God loves you and has a wonderful plan for your life."

> "I asked Jesus, 'How much do you love me?'
> And Jesus said, 'This much.'
> Then He stretched out His arms and died."
> – Unknown

God's love is meant to be experienced on a daily basis. We are meant to give and receive it as we tackle each new day. In Ruth 2:16, we read that Boaz instructed that "handfuls of purpose" be left for Ruth to find. Every day we should be looking for handfuls God has left, on purpose, just for us to discover. We should always be aware of His whispers of love in our daily life.

"Life is worth living, if life is about loving!" - Pastor Mark Smith

Reflections:

Are you living loved? Do you experience His love on a daily basis? Are you struggling with loneliness and isolation? God's presence is as near as a whisper. Be assured, God understands our need to love and to be loved. In Jeremiah 31:3, the prophet writes, *"The LORD hath appeared of old unto me, saying, Yea, I have loved thee with an everlasting love: therefore with lovingkindness have I drawn thee."* If you are willing to give and receive God's love and the love of others, He is ready and willing to supply you the opportunities to do so.

Ask Him today to meet your need to be loved. You will be amazed at the answer!

"Herein is love, not that we loved God, but that he loved us,

and sent his Son to be the propitiation for our sins."

1 John 4:10

CHAPTER THREE

Amazing Grace

God's Riches

In the last chapter, we discussed the love of God. We could say God's love is the WHY of salvation, and God's grace is the HOW of salvation. Grace, or **G**od's **R**iches **a**t **C**hrist's **E**xpense, is showing kindness to those who are utterly undeserving of such kindness. We see the wonder of God's grace in how desperately undeserving we, as its recipients, truly are and in how immeasurable are the riches bestowed upon us by His grace. Ephesians 2:4-7 tells us, *"But God, who is rich in mercy, for his great love wherewith he loved us, Even when we were dead in sins, hath quickened us together with Christ, (by grace ye are saved;) And hath raised us up together, and made us sit together in heavenly places in Christ*

Jesus: That in the ages to come he might shew the exceeding riches of his grace in his kindness toward us through Christ Jesus."

It is nearly impossible for us to comprehend the fact that there is nothing we can do to earn God's love, favor, and blessings; for salvation is, *"the gift of God: Not of works, lest any man should boast."*[28]

It is grace, and grace alone, that saves us! Sometimes, these verses are misquoted and read, "We are saved by faith." We are not saved by faith; we are saved *through* faith. Faith is the key that unlocks the door to God's grace![29]

Luke 7:37-38 tells the story of a woman who experienced God's grace in such a phenomenal way, we sing about it today:

"And, behold, a woman in the city, which was a sinner, when she knew that Jesus sat at meat in the Pharisee's house, brought an alabaster box of ointment, And stood at his feet behind him weeping, and began to wash his feet with tears, and did wipe them with the hairs of her head, and kissed his feet, and anointed them with the ointment."

In another verse we are told that the ointment she used was worth 300 pence. A pence was a day's wages. What could prompt a woman to devote almost a year's wages while humbling herself before a crowd of Pharisees, to wash and anoint the feet of the Savior? The Lord explains in verse 47, *"Wherefore I say unto thee, Her sins, which are many, are forgiven; for she loved much:*

---

28   Ephesians 2:8-9
29   Romans 5:2

but to whom little is forgiven, the same loveth little." Those who recognize their extreme poverty and helplessness are the most grateful for God's grace and favor upon their lives.

The Apostle Paul, having persecuted the church, was especially conscious of God's grace in his life. *"For I am the least of the apostles, that am not meet to be called an apostle, because I persecuted the church of God. But by the grace of God I am what I am: and his grace which was bestowed upon me was not in vain; but I laboured more abundantly than they all: yet not I, but the grace of God which was with me."*[30]

Julia Johnston expressed her wonder at God's grace in her song,

"Grace Greater than Our Sin"

Julia H. Johnston 1910

Marvelous grace of our loving Lord,

Grace that exceeds our sin and our guilt!

Yonder on Calvary's mount outpoured,

There where the blood of the Lamb was spilled.

Refrain:

Grace, grace, God's grace,

Grace that will pardon and cleanse within;

Grace, grace, God's grace,

Grace that is greater than all our sin!

---

30   1 Corinthians 15:9-10

Sin and despair, like the sea waves cold,

Threaten the soul with infinite loss;

Grace that is greater, yes, grace untold,

Points to the refuge, the mighty cross.

Dark is the stain that we cannot hide;

What can we do to wash it away?

Look! There is flowing a crimson tide,

Brighter than snow you may be today.

Marvelous, infinite, matchless grace,

Freely bestowed on all who believe!

You that are longing to see His face,

Will you this moment His grace receive?

There's a story of a prince who lived as a pauper, until one day it was discovered the pauper was actually the prince, heir to the entire kingdom. He'd lived in poverty without even enough food to eat, much less clothes to wear and shelter from the cold. Suddenly, he found himself arrayed in the finest apparel, sleeping in a luxurious bed, eating the best of meals, his every desire immediately met. Don't you wonder how long it would take for the reality to sink in?

There was an adopted little girl. She also had lived in great poverty. Her adopted parents were thrilled to have a little girl to love. They prepared a lovely room for her, with a canopy bed, all decked in frilly lace. That first night, they lovingly tucked her in and told her good night. In the morning, when they tiptoed in to check on her, they found her sleeping on the floor! She needed time to accept and acclimate to the change in her circumstances.

We are like that pauper-turned-prince and that adopted little girl. If we have lived beneath our privileges for too long, in poverty and despair, we find it difficult to accept the fullness of the riches that are ours in Christ.

How do we come to recognize and accept our true riches in Christ? There are two steps. First, we must believe and next, we must receive. If you never look at your bank balance, you never know how much you have in your account. There are many verses in the Bible that tell us how much we have in our accounts.

Ephesians 1:7 and 18 tell us, *"In whom we have redemption through his blood, the forgiveness of sins, according to the riches of his grace ...The eyes of your understanding being enlightened; that ye may know what is the hope of his calling, and what the riches of the glory of his inheritance in the saints."*

1 Peter 1:4 describes our inheritance, as believers, as, *"incorruptible, and undefiled, and that fadeth not away, reserved in heaven for us."*

When I read promises like these, I underline and highlight them in my Bible. I also like to memorize verses that remind me of the riches that are mine in Christ. If I am feeling a little down or discouraged, these truths cheer and encourage me. Affirmations can also help to encourage us.

Affirmations are clear statements of truth. They are declarations of what we believe by faith. Affirmations help us realize the riches God has bestowed upon us, by His grace. We claim the promises of God when we make affirmations based on the truths of God's Word. The next time you are feeling down or a little discouraged, read this list out loud. Your heart will quickly lift in praise for all the riches of His grace!

"I have found grace in the eyes of the Lord."

Genesis 6:8, Ruth 2:10

"I am justified freely by His grace."

Romans 3:24

"I am abounding in the grace of God."

2 Corinthians 8:7

"By His grace I am able to abound in every good work."

2 Corinthians 9:8, Ephesians 2:10

"The grace of God is sufficient for me."

2 Corinthians 12:9

"I am accepted in the beloved by His grace."

Ephesians 1:6

"I have forgiveness of sins, according to the riches of His grace."

Ephesians 1:7

"God shows the exceeding riches of His grace in His kindness toward me."

Ephesians 2:7

"I am given grace according to the measure of the gift of Christ."

Ephesians 4:7

"God has called me, according to His purpose and grace."

2 Timothy 1:9

"I have everlasting consolation and good hope through grace."

2 Thessalonians 2:16

"I am justified by His grace, and I am an heir according to the hope of eternal life."

Titus 3:7

"I come boldly unto the throne of grace, obtain mercy, and find grace to help in time of need."

Hebrews 4:16

"My heart is established with grace."

Hebrews 13:9

"When I am humble, God gives more grace to me."

James 4:6, I Peter 5:5

"I am growing in grace, and in the knowledge of our Lord and Savior Jesus Christ."

2 Peter 3:18

Reflections:

Are you still trying to earn God's love and approval? The remarkable changes God makes in our lives should be ample evidence of His love and acceptance. The song "Amazing Grace," written by a redeemed slave trader, John Newton, begins, "I once was lost and now am found, was blind and now I see." Here we see the great contrast between our old life and the new life God has given us, by His amazing grace.

Can you list some of the changes God has brought about in your own life? Here's a list to get you started.

Lost — Found

Blind — Seeing

Impoverished — Wealthy

Bound — Freed

Weak — Strong

Fearful —Confident

Rejected — Accepted

Sin-Sick — Whole

Defeated — Victorious

Despised — Beloved

As you read your Bible, start your own list of all of the riches God has bestowed upon you. Thank and praise God, every day, for your abundance in Christ. I guarantee you will be amazed!

"For the LORD God is a sun and shield:

the LORD will give grace and glory:

no good thing will he withhold from them that walk uprightly."

Psalm 84:11

CHAPTER FOUR

Amazing Answers

God's Response

There is nothing more thrilling than living a life of expectation, confident that God hears and answers our prayers. This is the essence of living a fulfilled, victorious Christian life. Normal Christian living is a life of power and answered prayers. If we are not experiencing answered prayer, we are living a powerless life. Sadly, there are Christians among us who have *"a form of godliness, but deny the power thereof."*[31] Often, people stop praying because they see no answers. Let's address the barriers to answered prayer.

We do not have, because we do not ask.[32]

---

31   2 Timothy 3:5
32   James 4:3

Prayer requires effort, determination, and discipline. We must dedicate a time, a place, and a list to our conversation with our Lord. When children are small and our schedules are hectic, it is sometimes difficult to find any time to ourselves, much less set aside a specific time and place to pray. When my children were small, my place of prayer was the couch in our living room. After my children and husband were asleep in bed, I would creep out to the couch, hugging my Bible. I kept my prayer list tucked into my Bible. There, I read and prayed and found the strength I needed.

Some prayers are answered before we even voice them. Others are not answered for years. Prayer lists help us to remember our requests and to keep praying. Persistent prayers are valuable, *"And I say unto you, Ask, and it shall be given you; seek, and ye shall find; knock, and it shall be opened unto you."*[33] The writer uses the progressive verb tense in this scripture, which means we are to ask and keep on asking, seek and keep on seeking, knock and keep on knocking. It is exciting when prayers are answered, and we mark them off of our lists. It is even more exciting when, after years of faithful asking, knocking, and seeking, our prayers are answered with a resounding, "Yes!"

I was deeply moved by a young pastor who spoke at a meeting I attended. I was thoroughly impressed by his sincerity and compassion, so I decided to add him to my prayer list. I could not remember his name, so I just called him "that young preacher." Over the next several years, I prayed for him often.

33   Luke 11:9

Almost 20 years later, I began attending a new church. The Pastor seemed familiar, but it was several years before I would make the connection. Eventually, his wife and I began talking about a meeting we had both attended, and suddenly, the pieces fell into place. The young preacher I had added to my list, so many years earlier, was now my own dear Pastor!

Life has changed. My children are all grown. I have much more time to myself, but somehow, life is still hectic and I need a prayer list now more than ever. My prayer list is now digital. It is available to me on my phone, computer and tablet. This allows me to stop and pray almost anytime and anywhere, and it allows me to add to my prayer list as things come to mind. I would not want to miss documenting even one amazing answer.

The most mind-blowing things happen to those who pray consistently! They experience ongoing answers to prayer. The power of God flows through their lives like a river.

Not asking in faith is yet another barrier to answered prayer.

Most Christians do believe God *can* answer prayer. They just do not believe He *will* answer prayer and in particular, their prayer. If our prayers are not answered, what is the point of praying? If we don't believe God will answer prayer, we don't ask. It becomes a hit-or-miss exercise. And if we are not in prayer regularly, we do not regularly experience answered prayer. Our faith is weak, because we are not living a life filled with the miraculous.

James 1:6-7 instructs us to, *"ask in faith, nothing wavering. For he that wavereth is like a wave of the sea driven with the wind and tossed. For let not that man think that he shall receive any thing of the Lord."* Faith must accompany our requests, because, according to Hebrews 11:6, *"without faith it is impossible to please him: for he that cometh to God must believe that he is, and that he is a rewarder of them that diligently seek him."*

As Christians, we must mature spiritually to where we not only believe God can answer prayer, but that we know He answers our prayers. *"And this is the confidence that we have in him, that, if we ask any thing according to his will, he heareth us: And if we know that he hear us, whatsoever we ask, we know that we have the petitions that we desired of him."*[34]

God does not answer our prayer because of who we are, but because of Who He is! The basic element of answered prayer is a relationship; a sweet, personal, intimate relationship with a loving, faithful, caring Father. If God is our Father, how can we doubt that He listens to us and answers our prayers?

Another barrier to answered prayer comes about when we do not ask according to the will of God.

"Ye ask, and receive not, because ye ask amiss, that ye may consume it upon your lusts"[35]

"And whatsoever we ask, we receive of him, because we keep his commandments, and do those things that are pleasing in his

---

34   1 John 5:14-15,
35   James 4:3

sight. And this is his commandment, That we should believe on the name of his Son Jesus Christ, and love one another, as he gave us commandment."[36]

"And be not conformed to this world: but be ye transformed by the renewing of your mind, that ye may prove what is that good, and acceptable, and perfect, will of God."[37]

When our minds are renewed and transformed, we come to understand what is the will of God. The basis of answered prayer is asking according to His will. So how can we address the will of God, in prayer?

Ask God to do His will.

Jesus taught us to pray, in Matthew 6:10, *"Our Father which art in heaven, Hallowed be thy name. Thy kingdom come. Thy will be done in earth, as it is in heaven."*

Why do we imagine that God's will for us is so contrary to our own will? A missionary confessed imagining God would call him to the deepest, darkest corner of Africa. He was afraid to pray for God's will, because he did not want to go to Africa. After years of resistance, he was offered an opportunity to travel to Zambia. Of course, he fell in love with the people and the place. He was then eager to pray for God's will to be done. His one regret was that he did not respond, sooner.

---

36   1 John 3:22-23
37   Romans 12:2

Praying for God's will to be done does not mean our hearts will not long for a particular answer or outcome. Yes, we must give up our own way, but in doing so, we discover amazing joy.

Ask God for what your heart longs to receive.

We should realize that we do not always know the will of God in prayer. David prayed and fasted, asking God to heal his child, even though he had already been told the child would die. He prayed anyway. When the child died, David said, *"While the child was yet alive, I fasted and wept: for I said, Who can tell whether GOD will be gracious to me, that the child may live?"*[38]

Jesus also prayed, knowing what awaited Him. He asked for the bitter cup to be removed, but ended by adding, *"not my will, but thine, be done."*[39]

As long as you have a desire, pray. Tell it to Jesus. God promises to give us the desires of our hearts. Pray until God answers or changes the desire of your heart. Remember to always have joy in your salvation, for the psalmist writes, *"Delight thyself also in the LORD; and he shall give thee the desires of thine heart."*[40]

Trust God, as long as it takes.

Many times, God answers our prayers before we even ask. He knows what we need. Other times, the answer to prayer is ongoing. God often reveals His will to us in seasons of quiet

---

38   2 Samuel 12:22
39   Luke 22:42
40   Psalm 37:4

expectation. We must, *"commit our way unto the LORD; trust also in him; and he shall bring it to pass."*[41]

When it seems that God is ignoring us or disregarding our requests, we should remember to, *"Wait on the LORD: be of good courage, and he shall strengthen thine heart: wait, I say, on the LORD."*[42]

We step outside the will of God when we refuse to wait. Consider the example of Abraham and Sarah. Abraham was 75 years old when God promised to make of him a great nation, in Genesis 12. At that point, it may have seemed possible that God would give him an heir. As time passed, Abraham's wealth and prestige multiplied, but no heir was born. In Genesis 15, Abraham suggests to God that maybe he should make his steward, Eliezer, his heir. God again promises Abraham a child of his own.

In Genesis 16, we find Sarah, ten years older and tired of waiting, devising her own plan. Since she is too old to have children, Abraham should have a child with her handmaid, Hagar. This was also not God's plan nor promise, and it proved to have devastating consequences.

Finally, fourteen years later (twenty-five since God first promised to make Abraham a great nation) Sarah conceived and bore a son. God fulfilled His promise, but in the meantime, Sarah and Abraham had made some poor choices trying to 'help' God do so.

---

41   Psalm 37:5
42   Psalm 27:14

Wait on the Lord. God is always good. God is always kind. God is always wise.

Trust God, regardless of the answer.

We are human. We are finite in understanding and knowledge. God is infinite. We cannot see the whole; He sees everything from beginning to ending. God reminds us, *"For my thoughts are not your thoughts, neither are your ways my ways, saith the LORD. For as the heavens are higher than the earth, so are my ways higher than your ways, and my thoughts than your thoughts."*[43]

There will be times when we want something so dearly, yet we must understand and accept that sometimes, the answer is "No." When our relationship with God is that of a child with her father, our desire is to see His will done. As a child, we ask our father, confidently, for all that we need. Many times, *not* having what we want is a greater blessing than the alternative. How many times did our earthly parents tell us no, because something was not good for us?

"No, that will spoil your dinner."

"No, that is not a good idea."

"No, it is time to go to bed."

After the disappointment comes the blessing.

Paul writes, in 2 Corinthians 12:8-10, *"For this thing I besought the Lord thrice, that it might depart from me. And he said unto*

---

43   Isaiah 55:8-9

me, My grace is sufficient for thee: for my strength is made perfect in weakness. Most gladly therefore will I rather glory in my infirmities, that the power of Christ may rest upon me. Therefore I take pleasure in infirmities, in reproaches, in necessities, in persecutions, in distresses for Christ's sake: for when I am weak, then am I strong."

As a child, it was necessary for me to have several surgeries. After being in the hospital the first time, I did not want to go back. It was strange and frightening and lonely. I remember sobbing to my father, begging him not to take me back there. And even all these years later, I remember his kindly telling me that I would never forgive them if they did not get this surgery for me. Of course, he was right, and I understand that now, but then it seemed like they were cruelly abandoning me. Remember, when the answer is "No," it is for our good and God's glory and one day, we will understand it all.

Waiting on God is much easier for me today than it was years ago. God has answered an enormous amount of prayers. I live with the confidence that God hears me when I pray, and I trust His answers when they come. I have been deeply disappointed on many occasions. I have wept bitter tears when I wanted the answer to be yes, and instead it was no. However, today, I can honestly say I rejoice in the no answers as well as the yes answers.

Confidence in God is another result of living an amazing Christian life. While it is true that *"faith cometh by hearing, and hearing by the Word of God,*"[44] once having exercised our faith, experiencing answers to prayer and God's promises fulfilled in our lives gives us even greater faith. We have confidence that others do not experience. Experience teaches us to trust and rely on Him, since, *"this is the confidence that we have in him, that, if we ask any thing according to his will, he heareth us:"*[45]

Reflections:

If you do not have a prayer list, I strongly encourage you to keep one. You not only need a prayer list to record your requests; you need a prayer list to record God's answers! God cares about your smallest concerns as well as your biggest. He delights in answering us when we pray.

---

44   Romans 10:17
45   1 John 5:14

"If ye abide in me, and my words abide in you,

ye shall ask what ye will, and it shall be done unto you."

John 15:7

CHAPTER FIVE

Amazing Truth

God's Revelation

This is a story. It is a love story – the very best kind of story. It has a beginning and middle, but no ending. It does not argue or cajole. It simply tells the story from a lover's point of view. Our story begins with God and His love letter to mankind.

Love letters are precious to the reader. They are personal. Love letters are intimate and speak to the heart of the beloved. And as anyone who has ever written a love letter knows, they are inspired; each word is chosen carefully and purposefully. Love letters are read and reread. They are treasured and carefully protected. They are often bundled and tucked away, and read again and again, year after year.

God has given to us His love letter, His Eternal Word. It is precious. It is personal. It speaks to our hearts. Every word has been chosen with care and purpose. It is meant to be treasured. It is meant to be read again and again, year after year.

There has always been a controversy concerning the veracity and accuracy of the Bible. Satan first planted doubt in Eve's mind in the Garden, when he asked her, *"Yea, hath God said?"*[46] And, today we ask, "How can we know that the Bibles we hold in our hands are the very words of God?" The answer lies in what the Bible says about itself. Consider these truths concerning God's Word.

The Word of God is an eternal Word.

The Word of God did not come into existence when men, moved of the Holy Ghost, began to pen it down.[47]

The Word of God did not come into existence when God took His finger and carved it into the stones on Mount Sinai.[48]

The Word of God did not come into existence when God spoke the first time to Abram. [49]

God's Word has always been from the beginning, for, *"By the word of the LORD were the heavens made; and all the host of*

---

46   Genesis 3:1
47   2 Peter 1:21
48   Exodus 31:18
49   Genesis 12:1

them by the breath of his mouth,"[50]. Jesus reminds us, *"Heaven and earth shall pass away, but my words shall not pass away."*[51]

If the Bible was not in existence until it was put into print, and if the only way the Bible could stay correct were if men preserved it, we would not have the ***eternal*** Word of God.

The written Word of God is an inspired Word.

Inspiration is a critical truth. The more you read your Bible, the more you will discover this. In Genesis 3:15, God gives a prophecy and then spends 65 books explaining that prophecy and its fulfillment. Over a period of 1500 years, over 40 authors wrote in three different languages: Greek, Hebrew, and Aramaic, a total of 66 books – 39 Old Testament and 27 in the New Testament – 1,189 chapters, 31,173 verses. For all of this diversity, throughout, there is one central message – Christ. The story follows line upon line, repeatedly, from the beginning to the end.

This is why we can't add to it and we can't take away from it. We cannot change it, because it is true. *"Every word of God is pure: he is a shield unto them that put their trust in him."*[52]

The written Word of God is a perfect Word.

Something that is perfect is without flaw. It is complete, with nothing missing. That is exactly how we can describe God's Word—flawless and complete. Have you ever heard someone

---

50   Psalm 33:6

51   Matthew 24:35

52   Proverbs 30:5

say, "I meant what I said, and I said what I meant?" God said it, and that settles it.

"For ever, O LORD, thy word is settled in heaven."[53]

The reality is very few people truly do say what they mean. Parents don't follow through on what they tell their children. Politicians don't follow through on their platforms. Teachers debate the rules with their students. It is no wonder that we have a difficult time believing God's Word is absolute, so much so that anyone who dares to say that the Bible is 100% correct is labeled a fanatic.

In the hearts and minds of numerous people, the promises of God are no more likely to be fulfilled than the promises of our political leaders.

Fortunately, God is not like man and *"His word is true from the beginning: and every one of his righteous judgments endureth for ever."*[54]

The written Word of God is a preserved Word.

It is a preserved Word; not preserved by men, but preserved by God. It is an act of God, not an act of man.

"The words of the LORD are pure words: as silver tried in a furnace of earth, purified seven times. Thou shalt keep them, O LORD, thou shalt preserve them from this generation for ever."[55]

---

53   Psalm 119:89
54   Psalm 119:160
55   Psalm 12:6-7

"The grass withereth, the flower fadeth: but the word of our God shall stand for ever."[56]

There is not one existing original Greek text in the world. All that we have are copies of copies of copies. Jesus never read from anything, but a copy. There was never a time in the Old or the New Testament, when all of the books of the Bible were assembled as one, and yet, they were all quoted as the Word of God. There has never been a time in history, when all of the originals were together, in one volume.

The Word of God is a living Word.

The Bible is a revelation of God. Creation is a revelation of God. Jesus Christ is a revelation of God. Jesus Christ did not come into existence in the manger; Jesus Christ has always existed. He is the One who spoke the Worlds into existence. He is the forerunner of all things. Consider the following scriptures:

"In the beginning was the Word, and the Word was with God, and the Word was God. The same was in the beginning with God. All things were made by him; and without him was not any thing made that was made. In him was life; and the life was the light of men."[57]

"And the Word was made flesh, and dwelt among us, (and we beheld his glory, the glory as of the only begotten of the Father, full of grace and truth."[58]

---

56   Isaiah 40:8
57   John 1:1-4
58   John 1:14

What is our conclusion?

With confidence, we can know that the authorized version of the Bible, which we hold in our hands, is the very Word of God. God has not allowed it to be corrupted. He does not need man to correct it.

Just because we don't completely understand every passage in the Bible, does not mean that what we can't grasp needs to be reinterpreted. It means we have learning and growing to do, before we can really "get" it. There are some things we are not meant to understand. Don't ever forget Whose Word it is! It is not the words of Moses. It is not the words of the prophets. It is not the words of Paul. It is not the words of the apostles. It is the Word of God!

There have always been pure copies of the Word of God. There have always been attempts to alter and pervert the message of the Bible. What the Bible says about itself, and the testimony of its impact on countless lives, is the best answer to its critics.

The Bible is not just a book. It is not a textbook or a newspaper to be skimmed and set aside. It is not text messaging, full of abbreviations and emojis. It is God's miraculous communication with man. It is a love letter, full of depth and nuances of meaning. It is a sword, a fire, a rock, a lamp, and it is truth! God's Word transforms lives.

Over the past 50 years (yes, I said 50) there has rarely been a day when I did not read my Bible. I am not sure how many times I have read it through, cover-to-cover, but it has been dozens of times. Like a tree drawing up water through its roots, I am strengthened, encouraged, directed, corrected, comforted, inspired, educated and so much more, as I absorb His Words into my heart. And like the wise man who built his house upon the rock, when the storms of life come (and they do), I am equipped to face them.

Reflections:

The greatest thing anyone can do to strengthen his or her faith is to read the Bible. One thing all great men and women of faith have in common is their love for God's Word.

To fill your heart and mind with His Word, read it every day. Read it out loud. Memorize it. Quote it. Write it. And above all else, allow it to convict, correct, and comfort you!

"Being born again, not of corruptible seed, but of incorruptible,

by the word of God, which liveth and abideth for ever."

1 Peter 1:23

Amazing Calling

God's Anointing

We have talked about amazing salvation, amazing love, amazing grace, amazing answers, and amazing truth, and certainly all of these are absolutely amazing. The limits of our understanding are exceeded when we ponder the wonder of these truths. The very thought of God so caring for us is certainly overwhelming, but now, the realization that beyond all of this God calls to each of us amazes us all the more.

God calls us to salvation.

"Come unto me, all ye that labour and are heavy laden, and I will give you rest."[59]

---

59   Matthew 11:28

God likens Himself to a bridegroom, and His Church to a bride. Just as the bridegroom pursues his bride with gentle words and sweet whispers of love, God calls to us. He calls us His beloved, and invites us to come with Him.[60]

Do you remember the first time you took your mate's hand? I do! He reached out his hand to me and I put mine in his. I never got tired of holding his hand. Sometimes we held hands watching TV. Sometimes we held hands walking together. Sometimes we held hands waiting in hospital rooms. It did not matter where we were, holding hands meant we were together.

God calls us to come to Him and walk with Him. He calls us to an intimate, deeply personal relationship with Him. One of, if not the very saddest, stories in life is that of unrequited love. God loves us and our response is, of course, to come to Him.

God calls us to honor and glorify Him with our lives. God has a plan for our lives. We were created for a divine purpose.

A calling could be defined as a profession, an occupation, an anointing, a mission or a commission. We are all included in the Great Commission, which implores us to *"Go ye therefore, and teach all nations, baptizing them in the name of the Father, and of the Son, and of the Holy Ghost:"[61]*

Once we are saved, our purpose in life should be to fulfill this Great Commission. Jesus gave it to all of us, not just a few of us. This does not mean that we should sell everything we own,

---

60   Song of Solomon 2:10
61   Matthew 28:19

pack up our families, and head to Botswana. It may mean that to some of us, but certainly not all of us! What it does mean, for all of us, is that God will guide us as individuals, to accomplish our part in fulfilling the Great Commission.

"For who will hearken unto you in this matter? but as his part is that goeth down to the battle, so shall his part be that tarrieth by the stuff: they shall part alike."[62] Some people go, and some people send. Let me reiterate, those who stay by the stuff are no less important or rewarded than those who go to the field.

God calls us where we are now.

"For whosoever shall call upon the name of the Lord shall be saved. How then shall they call on him in whom they have not believed? and how shall they believe in him of whom they have not heard? and how shall they hear without a preacher? And how shall they preach, except they be sent? as it is written, How beautiful are the feet of them that preach the gospel of peace, and bring glad tidings of good things!"[63]

Sometimes, because we are not the ones sent, we feel we have no calling, or we cannot see the significance of our calling. *"The eyes of your understanding being enlightened; that ye may know what is the hope of his calling, and what the riches of the glory of his inheritance in the saints."*[64]

---

62   1 Samuel 30:24
63   Romans 10:13-15
64   Ephesians 1:18

The person who cleans the toilets and sweeps the floors is just as called as the one who stands behind the pulpit. The person who changes diapers in the nursery is just as called as the one who teaches children in the jungle village. The one who goes to Boeing every day is just as called as the one who goes to Bulgaria for a lifetime. All of these actions are anointed by God, *"Who hath saved us, and called us with an holy calling, not according to our works, but according to his own purpose and grace, which was given us in Christ Jesus before the world began."*[65]

Every day, as we clean our house, or as we sit in traffic commuting to work, we must realize this is God fulfilling His calling in our lives. David sat on a hillside, watching his father's sheep. Not very glamorous, not very significant in others' eyes, but it was all a part of God's plan for his life. Ruth gleaned barley in the heat of the day. Her hands were red and rough, and her back ached by the time she returned home, but it was all a part of God's plan for her life.

Maybe at this moment, you do not see where God's plan is leading you. Maybe you do not feel a great empowerment as you quietly serve in your place; but if you are walking in His Spirit, if you are yielding to that still small voice, you can be assured that He has called you to such a time as this. Our circumstances have no bearing on God's calling.

Many times, I have heard ladies say, "I cannot serve God because I am divorced, because I am too old, because I am too young, because I am too weak, because I have to work, because my kids

---

65   2 Timothy 1:9

are too young." These reasons are merely excuses in God's realm, since, *"God hath distributed to every man, as the Lord hath called every one, so let him walk. And so ordain I in all churches."*[66]

No matter what your circumstances, God will use you, if you would just allow Him to do so.

Have you ever heard it said, "The greatest ability is availability?" Paul said, in 2 Corinthians 12:10, *"When I am weak, then am I strong."* God does not call us because of our talent, intellect, wealth, or beauty. God calls us because of our desire for Him. God will make useful, for His kingdom, whomever he desires, *"For ye see your calling, brethren, how that not many wise men after the flesh, not many mighty, not many noble, are called:"*[67]

The calling of God on our lives does not mean our lives will always be rosy. Our circumstances do not change God's plans. Many times, it is when we have reached the end of ourselves that we hear His voice the clearest, *"For the LORD hath called thee as a woman forsaken and grieved in spirit, and a wife of youth, when thou wast refused, saith thy God."*[68]

Just because things do not turn out the way we imagined they would, does not mean that He is not working in and through our circumstances.

Be prepared to respond to God's call.

---

66   1 Corinthians 7:17
67   1 Corinthians 1:26
68   Isaiah 54:6

The Christian life is an adventure. We should live a life of expectancy. Every morning, when we pick up our Bibles, we should think, "What will God show me today from His Word?" Every time we walk out of our front door, we should wonder, "Where will He lead me today?" With every opportunity that opens before us, we should ask, "How can the Lord work through me in this situation?"

Be prepared to respond by spending time in His Word.

If we are open, if we are expectant, God will direct our paths, God's Word is, *"a lamp unto our feet, and a light unto our path."*[69] Sometimes, God's desire for our lives starts with a suggestion; sometimes it is just a notion or idea that comes to us. Then, as we read His Word, a verse pops out at us. Perhaps it's a verse we've read many times before, but this time it's personal, like God is speaking directly to us, using the verse to direct our paths.

Waiting on the Lord to confirm His leading is always an important measure. Many factors can affect your decisions, emotions not being the least of these. There is wisdom in the old adage, "Sleep on it."

Be prepared to respond by seeking Him in prayer.

God is available to us, and we are to, *"Seek ye the LORD while he may be found, call ye upon him while he is near."*[70]

---

69   Psalm 119:105
70   Isaiah 55:6

Many times, we don't ask God for anything more than what Bill Gates could do for us. God wants to do great and mighty things, in and through our lives. Our part is to simply ask Him to use us, and then be sensitive and obedient to His answer. *"Call unto me, and I will answer thee, and shew thee great and mighty things, which thou knowest not."*[71]

When we resist the calling of God, our lives stall. When we respond to the calling of God, we become vessels, fit for the Master's use. Our lives become the greatest adventures imaginable. It does not matter how old, how smart, how talented, how educated, how articulate, how charming, how beautiful we may be. All that matters is our response to Him. Once surrendered, we can rest assured that our God, Who has called us, is faithful and will carry out His plans for us to completion.[72]

Reflections:

I had a friend who said every time her pastor preached on a need, she felt called to meet that need. Obviously, she could not be called to every foreign field and every ministry opportunity, but she had a tender heart that was ready to serve. The next time a need is presented, will you also be so tender and ready to respond? Take a bold step, and ask God to show you His calling. If you think you are called, but not really certain, write down your thoughts, and ask God to confirm them, or remove them. The answer will be amazing!

---

71   Jeremiah 33:3
72   1 Thessalonians 5:24

"And the Spirit and the bride say, Come.

And let him that heareth say, Come.

And let him that is athirst come.

And whosoever will, let him take the water of life freely."

Revelation 22:17

CHAPTER SEVEN

Amazing Fruit

God's Abundance

Many books have been written, many messages have been preached, and many songs have been sung about the abundant, fruitful life. The Lord does not want us to say, "Having an abundant, fruitful life would be amazing." He wants us to be able to say, "Wow! My life is amazing! God has given me an abundantly fruitful life!"

Jesus said, *"I am come that they might have life, and that they might have it more abundantly."*[73] God intends for all of us to experience abundantly fruitful lives. He has provided this for us. Sadly, not all of us choose an abundant life. Just like salvation, abundant living is a choice.

---

73   John 10:10

All of us can point to moments of decision that changed our lives forever. One of those moments is when we recognize our great need, and receive Jesus Christ as our Lord and Savior. There are also other life-changing decisions, when we commit ourselves to something or someone.

Marriage is also one of those life-changing decisions when, at some point we realize we have met the person with whom we want to spend the rest of our lives. It may have dawned on us gradually, or it may have struck like a thunderbolt! Either way, we are so certain, we are willing to pledge our entire lives to them.

Then, there are the moments when we commit our lives to a calling or purpose greater than ourselves. In my own life, I so clearly recall watching a made-for-TV movie entitled, "Green Eyes." It was the story of the orphans in Vietnam, after the war. I recall being struck with the hopelessness of any life without Christ. With a broken heart, I asked the Lord to please use me to reach this sad, sin-sick world. I told the Lord I would go anywhere and do anything He asked. It was a life-changing decision.

I was a young mother with two small children, and pregnant with a third. What could I do? I did not know, but I knew I would do whatever the Lord allowed me to do. *"Commit thy way unto the LORD; trust also in him; and he shall bring it to pass."*[74]

Apart from the moment I received Christ as my Lord and Savior, this moment has had the greatest impact on my life, even greater

---

74   Psalm 37:5

than marriage. Many times, the Lord has brought it back to me. "Remember when you said, anything?" He asks.

Did God send me to the mission field? No. Did God lead me into full-time ministry? No. Did God direct me to Bible College? No. God directed me to serve Him where I was, to live each and everyday representing Him, rejoicing in Him, hoping in Him, living for Him.

As a result, my life has been an adventure! Since I am almost always willing, and almost always expecting opportunities to open up before me, I get opportunities. Most times, when we think of abundant fruit, we think of earthly goods and riches. And truly, I have been abundantly blessed in this area. Almost anyone living in America has! But, abundant fruit means so much more. Abundant fruit bearing goes far, far beyond earthly wealth.

Writing this book has brought to mind the many exciting opportunities God has allowed me, over the years. You would be correct to say that I did not make any of these things happen. Rather than my making them happen, they happened to me. I was simply in the right place, at the right time, with the right people. To me, it is almost as if I am looking through a window at someone else's life. I am not the doer of these accomplishments; I am merely the observer of what God accomplishes. The experience is much like someone who plants a garden. Yes, the gardener may have tilled the ground and planted and watered the seeds, but God is the One who grew the flowers. I opened my heart and kept it tender; He has done the rest. The results are astounding.

You may think that keeping a tender heart is an easy task. It is not. It brings much, much pain. In our flesh, we are tempted to close our hearts, and protect ourselves.

I once had a dear friend who was discouraged in the ministry; he had been betrayed and deeply hurt by those he loved. He was at the point of quitting. I asked him, "Do you remember when you said, 'Anything, Lord?'" Quitting is never an option when you have said, "Anything, Lord."

This commitment requires a death to self will and self desires, but in exchange we become fruitful. *"Verily, verily, I say unto you, Except a corn of wheat fall into the ground and die, it abideth alone: but if it die, it bringeth forth much fruit."*[75]

Not everyone makes such a commitment and not everyone bears equal amounts of fruit. The parable Jesus told of the sower and the seed in Mark 4 explains this:

"Hearken; Behold, there went out a sower to sow: And it came to pass, as he sowed, some fell by the way side, and the fowls of the air came and devoured it up.

And some fell on stony ground, where it had not much earth; and immediately it sprang up, because it had no depth of earth: But when the sun was up, it was scorched; and because it had no root, it withered away.

And some fell among thorns, and the thorns grew up, and choked it, and it yielded no fruit.

---

75   John 12:24

And other fell on good ground, and did yield fruit that sprang up and increased; and brought forth, some thirty, and some sixty, and some an hundred... The sower soweth the word.

And these are they by the way side, where the word is sown; but when they have heard, Satan cometh immediately, and taketh away the word that was sown in their hearts.

And these are they likewise which are sown on stony ground; who, when they have heard the word, immediately receive it with gladness; And have no root in themselves, and so endure but for a time: afterward, when affliction or persecution ariseth for the word's sake, immediately they are offended.

And these are they which are sown among thorns; such as hear the word, And the cares of this world, and the deceitfulness of riches, and the lusts of other things entering in, choke the word, and it becometh unfruitful.

And these are they which are sown on good ground; such as hear the word, and receive it, and bring forth fruit, some thirtyfold, some sixty, and some an hundred."[76]

Notice from this parable that the only work the heart must do is to receive the seed and remain open to it. Fruit bearing is a natural process, just as natural as it is in a garden for flowers to grow from the seeds, planted by the gardener. Spiritual fruit is supernatural. Our pride wants to believe that we can do something to earn God's blessing of a fruitful life. But, then it would not be amazing; it would only be natural.

---

76   Mark 4:3-8, 14-20

In bearing fruit, we fulfill our purpose. I have never met a Christian, living an amazing Christian life, who did not want to bear fruit. If we are not bearing fruit, it is an indication of the condition of our own hearts. Jesus told His disciples, *"Follow me, and I will make you fishers of men."*[77] Our part is to follow; His part is to make us fruitful.

If you are not bearing fruit, or as much fruit as you once did, it is time to break up the hardness of your heart. All of us, from time to time, need to allow the Word of God to "stir us up." We grow complacent and cold to the needs of others and to the heart of God. Jesus admonishes us to *"Lift up your eyes, and look on the fields; for they are white already to harvest."*[78] Jeremiah tells us that what we see affects our hearts.[79]

I keep a list of those whom I know need Christ. I call this my "sweetheart list." I pray for these people often. I pray for them to clearly understand the Gospel. I pray for the conviction and the wooing of the Holy Spirit in their hearts. I also seek opportunities to present the Gospel to them myself. You may be uncomfortable presenting the Gospel to others and therefore, reluctant to ask God for such an opportunity. God knows your fear. Ask Him to help you overcome these concerns. When we pray, God answers! He may send you a partner to go with you. He may lead you to write a letter or hand them a tract. We are all a team; therefore, winning others to Christ is a team effort. Paul explained that some plant, others water, and God gives the increase.

77   Matthew 4:19
78   John 4:35
79   Lamentations 3:5

"I have planted, Apollos watered; but God gave the increase. So then neither is he that planteth any thing, neither he that watereth; but God that giveth the increase. Now he that planteth and he that watereth are one: and every man shall receive his own reward according to his own labour. For we are labourers together with God: ye are God's husbandry, ye are God's building."[80]

A seed never bears fruit, unless it dies first. The part we do not like is dying. We are selfish creatures. We do not like to be inconvenienced or delayed. I am ashamed to admit how many opportunities I have missed, because I was too busy to respond to another's need. However, we must move past our discomfort and share Christ's love, so all who will receive can experience living the way Jesus died and rose for us to live.

Reflections:

Are you living an amazing life? Can you look around and be amazed at all of the opportunities God has given to you? Are you amazed at the fruit God has brought about, because of your own tender heart?

Make a list of people you believe God would have you influence for Christ. Pray for them daily and look for opportunities to help them send them cards, make visits to see them, give them a gift, call them on the phone, or whatever else would give you a window to serve them. The results will be amazing!

80　　1 Corinthians 3:6-9

"Herein is my Father glorified,

that ye bear much fruit; so shall ye be my disciples.

... Ye have not chosen me,

but I have chosen you, and ordained you,

that ye should go and bring forth fruit,

and that your fruit should remain:

that whatsoever ye shall ask of the Father in my name,

he may give it you."

John 15:8, 16

CHAPTER EIGHT

Amazing Communion

God's Presence

Have you ever tried to describe to someone else what it is like to commune with God? It is difficult. It is like trying to explain what a banana tastes like to someone who has never had a banana, or to explain what a sunset looks like to someone who is blind. If someone does not have their own personal walk with God, they cannot possibly understand what it is like to commune with Him.

It is a very personal experience. It is an intimate relationship, uniquely meant for us as individuals. The song, "In the Garden," comes close to describing this relationship:

"In the Garden"

C. Austin Miles, 1912

I come to the garden alone
While the dew is still on the roses
And the voice I hear falling on my ear
The son of God discloses.
Refrain:
And he walks with me and he talks with me
And he tells me I am his own
And the joy we share as we tarry there
None other has ever known.

He speaks and the sound of his voice is so sweet
The birds hush their singing
And the melody that he gave to me
Within my heart is ringing.

I'd stay in the garden with him
Though the night around me is falling
But He bids me go through the voice of woe
His voice to me is calling...

Communing with God is not about feelings. It is about knowing. Feelings are a result of what we know. To know God, we must spend time with God. He beckons us to, *"Be still, and know that I am God: I will be exalted among the heathen, I will be exalted in the earth."*[81]

---

81   Psalm 46:10

It is in the darkest hours, the saddest moments, the times when we are most alone, that we experience God on the deepest levels. When we come to the end of ourselves, we find that God Himself is there. Although, *"weeping may endure for a night, but joy cometh in the morning."*[82]

When we finally stop struggling in our own strength and wisdom, when we are finally willing to give up on our own plans and programs, we find God waiting to solve our dilemmas. It seems that we must exhaust all of our own resources before we are ready to experience the reality of God's power and presence. It is one thing to know about the promises of God. It is another to experience the fulfillment of those promises in our lives. No one can experience communion with the Father quite the same way that we can; that is why, *"it is good for me to draw near to God: I have put my trust in the Lord GOD, that I may declare all thy works."*[83]

Sadly, we have all known people who did not find God at their lowest points. Instead, they turned to something or someone else. We, as Christians, can do the same thing. Instead of trusting ourselves to our loving Lord, we trust our money, or our abilities, or our jobs. Israel did exactly this. The Lord reminded them, *"In returning and rest shall ye be saved; in quietness and in confidence shall be your strength: and ye would not."*[84]

---

82   Psalm 30:5
83   Psalm 73:28
84   Isaiah 30:15

It takes us time and maturity to come to the place where we recognize God's voice. Jesus said, *"My sheep hear my voice, and I know them, and they follow me."*[85]

The lesson of Elijah is an excellent example of this. Elijah was like all of us are at times. He had seen the mighty power of God. In answer to his prayer, God sent fire from heaven to consume a sacrifice and the wood, stones, and even the water that it was placed upon. But, even after seeing God's power in such a mighty way, Elijah ended up in a cave feeling alone and depressed, like his troubles were all too big for God.

God knew what Elijah needed. The Bible tells us, *"and a great and strong wind rent the mountains, and brake in pieces the rocks before the LORD; but the LORD was not in the wind: and after the wind an earthquake; but the LORD was not in the earthquake: And after the earthquake a fire; but the LORD was not in the fire: and after the fire a still small voice."*[86] And when Elijah heard the still, small voice, he knew it was God's voice, and he was encouraged.[87]

Sometimes, being still and waiting are the hardest things in the world. I don't know of anyone who likes to wait. But, this is exactly where we find God, in the waiting room. It may seem counter productive, but here again we must, *"Wait on the LORD: be of good courage, and he shall strengthen thine heart: wait, I say, on the LORD."*[88]

---

85   John 10:27
86   1 Kings 19:11-12
87   You can find the entire story in 1 Kings 18-19
88   Psalm 27:14

We learn **about** God as we study His Word and witness His wonderful works, but we learn **of** God when we spend time with Him, when we allow ourselves to be still and listen, when we rest in Him. Jesus said, *"Take my yoke upon you, and* **learn of me**; *for I am meek and lowly in heart: and ye shall find rest unto your souls."*[89] (Emphasis added) Jesus taught, *"And this is life eternal, that they might know thee the only true God, and Jesus Christ, whom thou hast sent."*[90]

This is the exact reason God sent His Son, that we might know Him! We were separated by sin and rebellion. God repaired the breach on the cross of Calvary and now invites us into a personal, intimate relationship with Him. Now we know that, *"But as many as received him, to them gave he power to become the sons of God, even to them that believe on his name."*[91]

Is there any sweeter earthly relationship than that of a father and a child? *And because ye are sons, God hath sent forth the Spirit of his Son into your hearts, crying, Abba, Father,"*[92] When we believe on His name, we become the sons of God. You may have heard it explained that the Greek word Abba is similar to our word Daddy, a sweet, intimate name that defines a cherished relationship.

As a firstborn, I was particularly close to my own father. I recall that when my little girl problems overwhelmed me, I would crawl onto my Daddy's lap where he would envelop me in his big arms.

---

89   Matthew 11:29
90   John 17:3
91   John 1:12
92   Galatians 4:6

There, I was safe. I was secure. My daddy seemed invincible. This is the comfort we find when we reach up to our heavenly Father, seeking His assurance and love.

"For I know whom I have believed, and am persuaded that he is able to keep that which I have committed unto him against that day."[93]

Reflections:

How's your communion with God? Do His words speak to you? Are you confident He hears when you pray? Is it easy and natural to express your love to Him? Are you comforted by His presence when life is difficult? Why not crawl up in His lap today, and tell Him everything? Confess how you have failed Him in trying to do things in your own strength. Tell Him about your sorrows and disappointments, and allow Him to heal the hurts.

---

93   2 Timothy 1:12

"Casting all your care upon him; for he careth for you."

1 Peter 5:7

CHAPTER NINE

Amazing Wisdom

God's Guidance

I particularly looked forward to writing this chapter. As you know by now, there are many things about the Christian life that amaze me. God granting me His wisdom and His guidance on a daily basis is certainly one of them; especially since I am keenly aware of my need in this area.

Have you ever thought back over a conversation and felt embarrassed or anxious over something you said? How many times are the things we say not taken as we meant them? As a public speaker this can be even more humiliating than it is in everyday conversation. It is a strong reminder of how much we need God's wisdom in even the most common of daily interactions.

I love and rely on the promise in the book of James, *"If any of you lack wisdom, let him ask of God, that giveth to all men liberally, and upbraideth not; and it shall be given him."*[94]

"If any of you lack wisdom?" That would be me! Have you ever been stuck for an answer, stymied by a situation? If there is anything life has taught me, it is that I don't know. I am afraid, that like so many other lessons in life, I learned this one the hard way.

I was hired to straighten out a company's books. There had been serious intermingling of funds. On top of that, in the midst of hopelessly tangling up the accounts, they changed software programs three times. "No problem!" I confidently told their CEO. It was a puzzle I was certain I could solve. For days, I sat in front of the computer. I printed stacks of papers. Every time I thought I had it figured out, a new account popped up. One day, I sat in the little accounting office and, weeping, I finally seriously prayed. Of course, I prayed during the entire process, but on this day, I truly recognized my need for God's great wisdom, so I begged for it. God's wisdom always trumps my own. *"Thus saith the LORD, Let not the wise man glory in his wisdom, neither let the mighty man glory in his might, let not the rich man glory in his riches,"*[95] Many times in life, we sprint forward, confident in our own wisdom and ability. Don't mistake what I am saying.

---

94   James 1:5
95   Jeremiah 9:23

We should have confidence, but not solely in our intellect, our education, or our abilities—not in ourselves. We should have confidence in God, Who gave us these assets. Above and beyond this, we should have confidence in the wisdom God will grant us if we ask. I am afraid we undervalue God's wisdom, along with His willingness to give it to us.

In 1 Kings 3, Solomon asks God to give him an understanding heart, so, *"God gave Solomon wisdom and understanding exceeding much, and largeness of heart, even as the sand that is on the sea shore. And Solomon's wisdom excelled the wisdom of all the children of the east country, and all the wisdom of Egypt."*[96]

How do we know when God is guiding? What a great question. Proverbs 3:5-6 is a good place to start. *"Trust in the LORD with all thine heart; and lean not unto thine own understanding. In all thy ways acknowledge him, and he shall direct thy paths."*

The key to this promise is recognizing when we are leaning on our own understanding, and when we are trusting in our own reasoning rather than allowing Him to direct our paths. t

When you are seeking God's guidance, earnestly try to set aside your own selfish wants. There are requests all of us would like God to grant but, we cannot honestly say that we know they are God's will. Sometimes God gives us a desire as He leads us in a particular direction. Other times, our desires are a result of our own wants and whims, and God knows they would hinder us if He granted them. At times like these, place your petition before

---

96   1 Kings 4:29-30

your loving and infinitely wise Lord and leave it there. "No" is also an answer to prayer.

Unfortunately, there have been too many times when I have pushed ahead demanding my own way and suffered the results of my foolish decisions.

My mother loved thrift stores, not only because she saved money, but she just loved sifting through thrift stores. My mother was one of the those thrift store shoppers who picks up each item, looks at it front and back, and then places it back on the rack. To a child, her perusing the racks seemed never ending, at least until I was old enough to flip through the racks myself.

On one of these shopping excursions, I came across a pair of red pants. You read that right. Red pants! Today, we would call them gauchos. Then, I suppose, we called them baggy. I loved those pants. I wanted those pants. My mother warned against those pants. But, for a quarter, I am sure she felt I could learn my lesson the hard way.

Now, when I was growing up, young ladies did not wear pants to school, as they were strictly intended for playing outside. So the next day, I donned my red pants and proudly wore them outside to play. The neighborhood boys immediately critiqued my fashion sense. "What are you wearing? You look like a clown!" Much to my chagrin, my treasured acquisition became known as my clown pants. Suddenly I did not love them anymore. As a matter-of-fact, I regretted them immensely. In short order, they made their way back from whence they came, and my respect for my mother's opinion increased exponentially!

Obviously, this lesson made a big impact on my thinking, since I remember it all these years later. A $0.25 pair of pants is not nearly as regrettable a decision as, perhaps, purchasing the wrong car or wrong house, or even marrying the wrong person. Before making any major decision, always seek counsel from those who have demonstrated godly wisdom in their own lives.

Sometimes, I genuinely do not know what to do about a situation. At these times, my pastor's advice is invaluable. One thing he always does is to help me apply the Word of God to my situation. We can never have genuine wisdom until we give God and His Word the proper respect and reverence, *"The fear of the LORD is the beginning of wisdom: a good understanding have all they that do his commandments: his praise endureth for ever."*[97]

The benefits of godly wisdom cannot be overstated. *"Through wisdom is an house builded; and by understanding it is established: ... So shall the knowledge of wisdom be unto thy soul: when thou hast found it, then there shall be a reward, and thy expectation shall not be cut off."* [98]

"For wisdom is better than rubies; and all the things that may be desired are not to be compared to it." [99]

---

97   Psalm 111:10
98   Proverbs 24:3, 14
99   Proverbs 8:11

We have heard it said, "Hindsight is 20/20." We can all probably look back on decisions we wish we hadn't made. Perhaps it was in haste, or maybe it was an urgent feeling that led us to say yes. As a women's leader, more than once women have told me that they do not care what the Bible says; God understands their hearts, and they are going to do what they want. And, yes, more than once they have come back to me and said, "I made a terrible mistake." God knows things we don't know. God sees things we can't see. Even when something seems so right, if it is contrary to God's Word it is wrong. *"Folly is joy to him that is destitute of wisdom: but a man of understanding walketh uprightly...The fear of the LORD is the instruction of wisdom; and before honour is humility."*[100]

If we ignore the basic principles of life, we suffer the inevitable consequences. Most of the time, when someone asks me for advice, the person asking already knows the answers. So many more times, I listen as someone tries to rationalize a decision they already know is the wrong decision. They refuse to take heed to the advice in Proverbs 22:23 that admonishes us to, *"Buy the truth, and sell it not; also wisdom, and instruction, and understanding."*

Not every decision is not black and white. After you have earnestly asked God for wisdom, sought out godly counsel, and applied God's Word to your situation, then you must trust God to direct your path.

---

100   Proverbs 15:21, 33

I research everything. I never make a major purchase until I have studied my options from every possible aspect. But sooner or later, a decision must be made and once it's done, we must trust that God has directed us. Again, from the book of James, we read, *"If any of you lack wisdom, let him ask of God, that giveth to all men liberally, and upbraideth not; and it shall be given him. But let him ask in faith, nothing wavering. For he that wavereth is like a wave of the sea driven with the wind and tossed. For let not that man think that he shall receive any thing of the Lord. A double minded man is unstable in all his ways."*[101] We must ask, in faith, for guidance, and once the decision is made, we should not second-guess ourselves or God.

We live in times plagued with instability. Just like a wobbly building, instability in a life, a community, a nation and the world arises when there is no firm foundation. Truth dictates that there must be absolutes. In a world where everything is relative, there is no stability. *"wisdom and knowledge shall be the stability of thy times, and strength of salvation: the fear of the LORD is his treasure."*[102]

I have made decisions I later regretted, but never when I first sought the will of God and obeyed His leading. There have been times when others were very much opposed to my decisions, but because I was certain of His leading (usually from His Word) I obeyed God. I can honestly say, I have never regretted a decision I made that was made in obedience to God. Jesus said, *"But*

---

101   James 1:5-8
102   Isaiah 33:6

wisdom is justified of all her children."[103] We might say, "The proof of the pudding is in the taste." Godly wisdom, when exercised, is always revealed by the results that follow.

"Who is a wise man and endued with knowledge among you? Let him shew out of a good conversation his works with meekness of wisdom." James 3:13

But the wisdom that is from above is first pure, then peaceable, gentle, and easy to be intreated, full of mercy and good fruits, without partiality, and without hypocrisy." James 3:17

Reflections:

Life is made up of the choices we make. Are you facing life-changing decisions? If not today, you will be facing them soon. Now is the time to seek the wisdom and guidance of the One Who sees both the beginning and the ending.

"God always gives His best to those who leave the choice with him." - Jim Elliot

---

103   Luke 7:35

"Get wisdom, get understanding: forget it not;

neither decline from the words of my mouth.

Wisdom is the principal thing; therefore get wisdom:

and with all thy getting get understanding."

Proverbs 4:5

CHAPTER TEN

Amazing Worship

Our Response

One afternoon, a Christian shared the wonderful plan of salvation with the man sitting beside him on an airplane. The man listened politely and then responded, "I don't believe in heaven or hell. I believe heaven and hell are here on earth." Thinking he had stumped the Christian, he was surprised by the kind response. "If that is the case, is your life on earth heaven or hell?"

As amazing and magnificent as it is to live for Christ, many are not enjoying their Christian lives fully. Our lives should be a taste of heaven on earth. Every day should bring with it little glimpses of eternity. God's presence in our lives should be real and personal, not because of who we are, but because of Who He is!

"When He Reached Down His Hand for Me," the famous song by Marion Easterling, expresses eloquently how helpless we are to rescue ourselves, and how willing and able our Savior is to bring us to Himself.

Once my soul was astray from the heavenly way.

I was wretched and vile as could be,

But my Savior in love, gave me peace from above

When he reached down His hand for me.

Genuine praise and worship are the results of realizing how truly amazing our own lives are in Christ. When we realize that our lives are not a result of our own works and goodness, but rather a result of His miraculous power; what else could a heart filled with this realization do, but pour out worship, praise, and adoration for the One who loves us so?

"Make a joyful noise unto the LORD, all ye lands. Serve the LORD with gladness: come before his presence with singing. Know ye that the LORD he is God: it is he that hath made us, and not we ourselves; we are his people, and the sheep of his pasture. Enter into his gates with thanksgiving, and into his courts with praise: be thankful unto him, and bless his name. For the LORD is good; his mercy is everlasting; and his truth endureth to all generations."[104]

This psalm describes four ways to praise our God. Let's look at each one, briefly.

---

104   Psalm 100:1-5

Praise in Song

"O sing unto the LORD a new song: sing unto the LORD, all the earth."[105] The reason the Bible speaks of a new song is because there is an old song. It is a sad, slow discouraging song. It is the song of the world in which we live and sometimes, even we Christians join in the chorus. The Bible tells us that all of creation groans because of the bondage of sin.[106] But God has given us a new song! It has new words and a new melody. It is a song of liberty and redemption. It is a song of thanksgiving and praise. When we see God for Who He is, we are able to join the psalmist and sing, *"And he hath put a new song in my mouth, even praise unto our God: many shall see it, and fear, and shall trust in the LORD."*[107]

There is something wrong if we do not have a song of praise in our hearts. It is an indication that we are more focused on ourselves, and the circumstances of this present world than we are on the God of our salvation and His goodness. Our thoughts must be set upon Him, and not upon ourselves. If we keep our minds on the Lord, He will keep us in perfect peace.[108] We will praise Him with fixed hearts,[109] and we will magnify Him with thanksgiving.[110]

---

105   Psalm 96:1
106   Romans 8:22
107   Psalm 40:3
108   Isaiah 26:3
109   Psalm 57:7
110   Psalm 69:30

Even those of us who cannot carry a tune can have a song in our hearts!

Praise in Service

Christmas is a special time of the year. We eagerly look forward to it at our house. Even though the children are all now adults, I still go overboard. I bake their favorite cookies and make their favorite dishes. The overflow of gifts under the tree spills out past the couch. Each year, I tell myself that I will cut back. They all have their own homes where they celebrate and in-laws' homes where they enjoy food and gifts also. But, for this old German gal, giving gifts and cooking meals is how we show love.

How can we say we love our God, if we have no desire to serve Him? Joyful service stems from the overflow of love, *"Serve the LORD with gladness: come before his presence with singing."*[111]

The Lord rebuked Satan when He said, *"Get thee hence, Satan: for it is written, Thou shalt worship the Lord thy God, and him only shalt thou serve."*[112]

Service, when it is given out of a full heart, is an act of praise, love and worship.

Praise in Sacrifice

In both the Old and New Testaments, we are told to bring the sacrifice of praise before the Lord:

---

111   Psalm 100:2
112   Matthew 4:10

"The voice of joy, and the voice of gladness, the voice of the bridegroom, and the voice of the bride, the voice of them that shall say, Praise the LORD of hosts: for the LORD is good; for his mercy endureth for ever: and of them that shall bring the sacrifice of praise into the house of the LORD. For I will cause to return the captivity of the land, as at the first, saith the LORD."[113]

"By him therefore let us offer the sacrifice of praise to God continually, that is, the fruit of our lips giving thanks to his name."[114]

Why would praise and thanksgiving be considered a sacrifice? As forgetful human beings, we tend to take all of God's goodness to us for granted. When things aren't going as we think they should go, we don't always want to acknowledge God's many blessings. You really cannot feel sorry for yourself while giving thanks and praise. Praising and thanking God helps us to remember the God of our salvation, and puts life into perspective.

"Praise ye the LORD. O give thanks unto the LORD; for he is good: for his mercy endureth for ever,"[115]

"Surely the righteous shall give thanks unto thy name: the upright shall dwell in thy presence."[116]

Praise in Eternity

---

113 Jeremiah 33:11
114   Hebrews 13:15
115 Psalm 106:1
116 Psalm 140:13

Heaven is a place of praise and worship. *"To the end that my glory may sing praise to thee, and not be silent. O LORD my God, I will give thanks unto thee for ever."*[117]

Heaven is where God is worshipped day and night, forever and ever. In the book of Revelation, the scene before the throne of God is described:

After this I beheld, and, lo, a great multitude, which no man could number, of all nations, and kindreds, and people, and tongues, stood before the throne, and before the Lamb, clothed with white robes, and palms in their hands; And cried with a loud voice, saying, Salvation to our God which sitteth upon the throne, and unto the Lamb. And all the angels stood round about the throne, and about the elders and the four beasts, and fell before the throne on their faces, and worshipped God, Saying, Amen: Blessing, and glory, and wisdom, and thanksgiving, and honour, and power, and might, be unto our God for ever and ever. Amen. [118]

Jesus said that if men would not praise Him, the stones themselves would cry out at His presence.[119]

Praising God is the very natural response to the amazing life He has given to us. *"Every day will I bless thee; and I will praise thy name for ever and ever. ... My mouth shall speak the praise of the LORD: and let all flesh bless his holy name for ever and ever."*[120]

Reflections:

117   Psalm 30:12
118   Revelation 7:9-12
119   Luke 19:40
120   Psalm 145:2,21

Sometimes, I try to write my own song of praise to the Lord. It doesn't take me long to find that my vocabulary is woefully inadequate. I have even gone so far as to start making lists of words to describe our God and my love and gratitude to Him. Why not try it yourself? God is pleased with praise, so pleased in fact, that the Bible tells us in Psalm 22:3, that He inhabits praise. Now that is amazing!

The LORD is my strength and my shield; my heart trusted in him, and I am helped: therefore my heart greatly rejoiceth; and with my song will I praise him.

Psalm 28:7

Reality Check

Your Christian life may be anything but amazing, and you may feel that this book has failed to address life in the real world. At this point, you may be a little disappointed, and even frustrated because you were looking for more answers to the complexities of life. You may be thinking that I am totally out of touch with the realities of living in this place, where evil is ever-present.

Let me assure you that I get it. I know about loss and heartache. I know about dark days, when getting out of bed seems to be an insurmountable task. Just like some of you, I know about days, weeks, and even months of walking like a zombie through hopelessness and depression. This is exactly why Jesus died for us. He died to deliver us from the ravages of sin. I know living an amazing Christian life is possible, because my own life has been transformed, and it is amazing!

Our Lord's purpose for coming is extraordinary; *"Who gave himself for our sins, that he might deliver us from this present evil world, according to the will of God and our Father:"*[121]

Once we enter into a living relationship with God through His Son, the Lord Jesus Christ, God has a wonderful plan for our lives. God's plan is to transform our lives. We are new creatures in Christ. *"Therefore if any man be in Christ, he is a new creature: old things are passed away; behold, all things are become new."*[122]

To learn more about living an amazing Christian Life, I encourage you to locate a Church where the Bible is taught and believed.

Our next book, based on a series by Pastor Mark Smith explores what it means to live and authentic Christian life, a miraculously changed life.

For more information on upcoming books and materials visit us at www.lastinglegacybooks.com. Sign up for e-mail updates while you are there.

If you would like a free New Testament with a series of lessons on living the Christian life, or help in locating a Bible believing church contact me at:

cynthia@lastinglegacybooks.com.

---

121   Galatians 1:4
122   2 Corinthians 5:17

Made in the USA
San Bernardino, CA
19 March 2017